CHRISTMAS FAVORITES

Solos and String Orchestra Arrangements
Correlated with Essential Elements String Method

Arranged by
LLOYD CONLEY

Welcome to Essential Elements Christmas Favorites! This book is designed to be used as a complement to the STRING ORCHESTRA arrangements. These easy percussion parts may be played by members of the string orchestra or by adding one or two percussion students.

ISBN 978-0-7935-8922-7

HAL•LEONARD®
CORPORATION
7777 W. BLUEMOUND RD. P.O. BOX 13819 MILWAUKEE, WI 53213

00868029

JINGLE BELLS

PERCUSSION
Sleigh Bells

Words and Music by J. PIERPONT
Arranged by LLOYD CONLEY

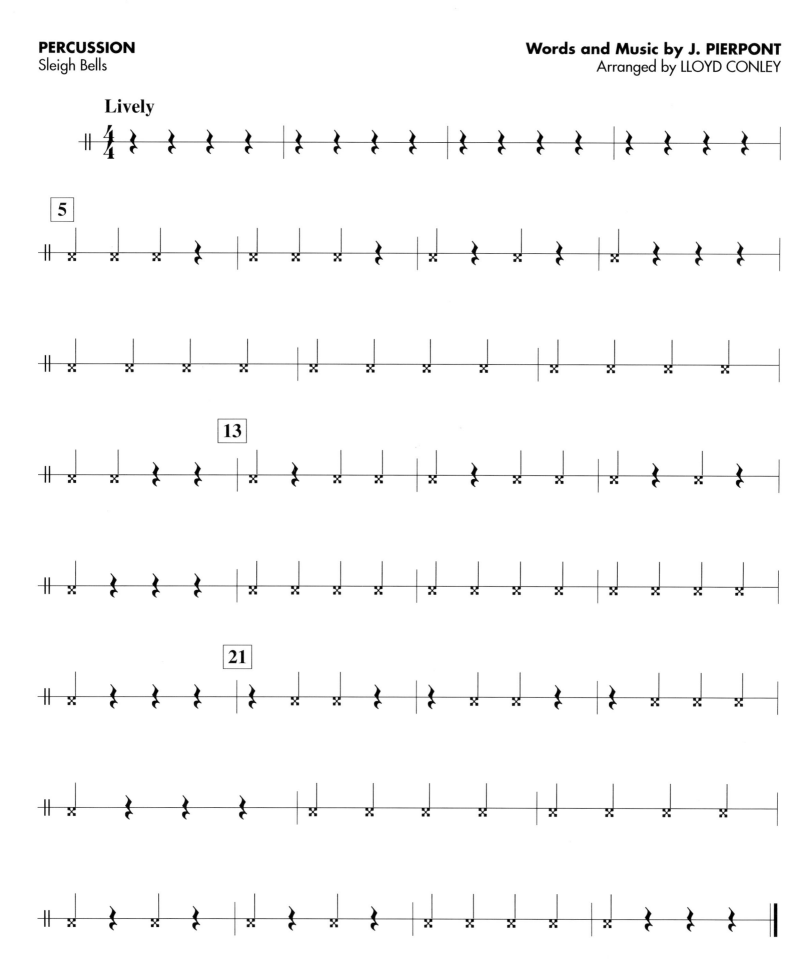

UP ON THE HOUSETOP

PERCUSSION
Wood Block, Sleigh Bells

Words and Music by B.R. HANDY
Arranged by LLOYD CONLEY

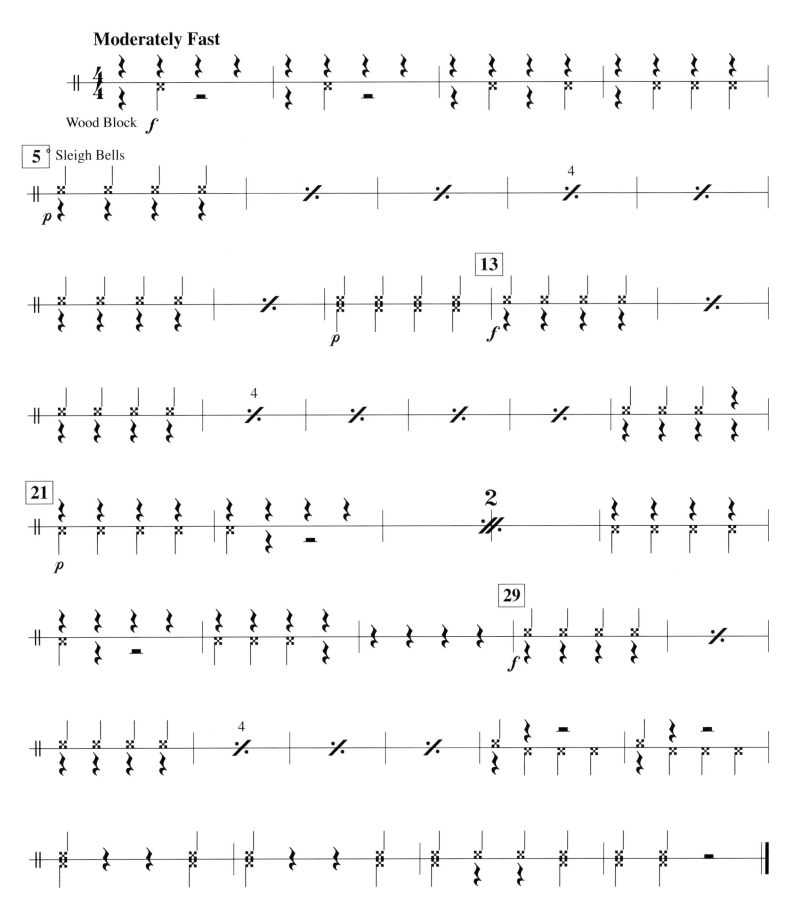

00868029

THE HANUKKAH SONG

PERCUSSION
Tambourine, Low Tom-Tom

Traditional
Arranged by LLOYD CONLEY

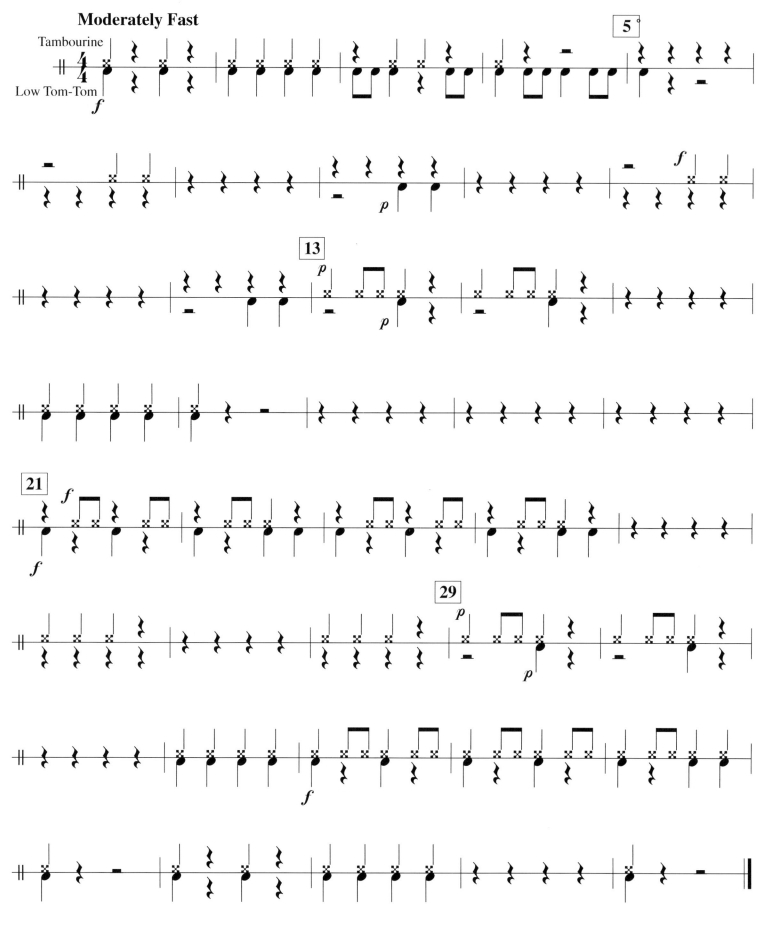

WE WISH YOU A MERRY CHRISTMAS

PERCUSSION 1 & 2
Wood Block, Bells

Traditional English Folksong
Arranged by LLOYD CONLEY

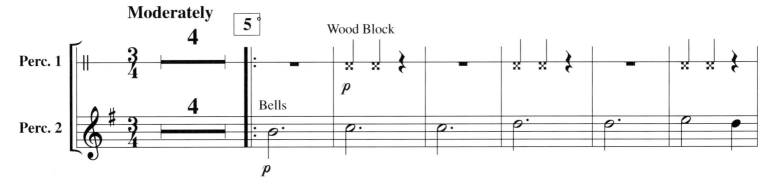

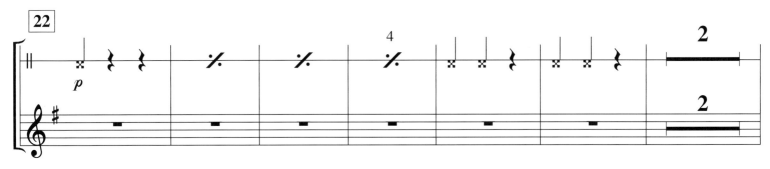

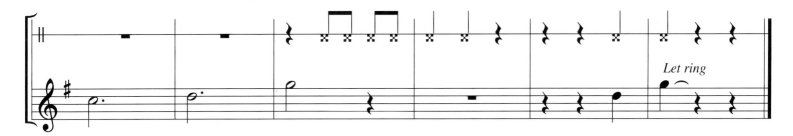

A HOLLY JOLLY CHRISTMAS

PERCUSSION 1 & 2
Sleigh Bells, Bells

Music and Lyrics by JOHNNY MARKS
Arranged by LLOYD CONLEY

00868029

FROSTY THE SNOW MAN

PERCUSSION
Sleigh Bells, Tom-Toms (2)

**Words and Music by
STEVE NELSON and JACK ROLLINS**
Arranged by LLOYD CONLEY

00868029

ROCKIN' AROUND THE CHRISTMAS TREE

PERCUSSION
Sleigh Bells, Wood Block

Music and Lyrics by **JOHNNY MARKS**
Arranged by LLOYD CONLEY

JINGLE-BELL ROCK

PERCUSSION 1 & 2
Sleigh Bells, Bells

**Words and Music by
JOE BEAL and JIM BOOTHE**
Arranged by LLOYD CONLEY

00868029

SILVER BELLS
From the Paramount Picture THE LEMON DROP KID

Words and Music by
JAY LIVINGSTON and RAY EVANS
Arranged by LLOYD CONLEY

BELLS

Moderately — freely

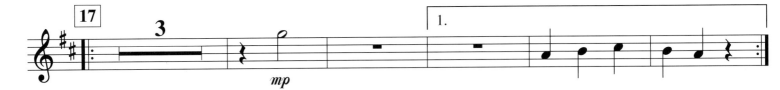

LET IT SNOW! LET IT SNOW! LET IT SNOW!

Words by SAMMY CAHN
Music by JULE STYNE
Arranged by **LLOYD CONLEY**

PERCUSSION
Triangle, Sleigh Bells

00868029

WHITE CHRISTMAS
From the Motion Picture Irving Berlin's HOLIDAY INN

**Words and Music by
IRVING BERLIN**
Arranged by LLOYD CONLEY

BELLS